PAPER CRAFTS

Meryl Doney

Gareth Stevens Publishing
A WORLD ALMANAC EDUCATION GROUP COMPANY

About this Book

The book in which you are reading these words is made entirely from paper and cardboard. We use these materials all the time, but we often take them for granted. Yet paper and cardboard have a very long and varied history. In this book, we trace the story of papermaking from earliest times. We also show you how to create handmade paper, using common materials and simple equipment. This is followed by some examples of the many ways of making and decorating paper items.

Throughout this book, maps show you where the various types of paper crafts come from. Each left-hand page describes a craft from one or more countries. Full-color photographs show items that have been made by native craftsmen. Each right-hand page provides step-by-step instructions, with illustrations, for making a paper item.

Most of the steps for making the projects in this book are easy to follow, but wherever you see this symbol, ask for help from an adult.

Measurement Conversions:

1 inch = 2.54 centimeters (cm)
1 inch = 25.4 millimeters (mm)
1 ounce = 29.5735 milliliters (ml)

Please visit our web site at: www.garethstevens.com
For a free color catalog describing Gareth Stevens Publishing's list of high-quality books and multimedia programs, call 1-800-542-2595 (USA) or 1-800-387-3178 (Canada). Gareth Stevens Publishing's fax: (414) 332-3567.

Library of Congress Cataloging-in-Publication Data

Doney, Meryl, 1942-
        Paper crafts/ by Meryl Doney.
            p. cm. — (Crafts from many cultures)
        Includes bibliographical references and index.
        Summary: Information about the history of paper and its uses accompanies instructions for making different types of papers and objects such as flowers, trays, lanterns, and more from paper.
        ISBN 0-8368-4046-1 (lib. bdg.)
        1. Paper work—Juvenile literature.   2. Paper, Handmade—Juvenile literature.   3. Decorative paper—Juvenile literature.   [1. Papermaking.   2. Paper work.   3. Handicraft.]   I. Title.
TT870.D63   2004
745.54—dc22   2003055858

This North American edition first published in 2004 by
Gareth Stevens Publishing
A World Almanac Education Group Company
330 West Olive Street, Suite 100
Milwaukee, Wisconsin 53212 USA

This U.S. edition copyright © 2004 by Gareth Stevens, Inc.
Original edition copyright © 1997 by Franklin Watts.
Text © 1997 by Meryl Doney.

First published as *World Crafts: Papercraft* in 1997 by Franklin Watts, 96 Leonard Street, London WC2A 4XD, England. Additional end matter copyright © 2004 by Gareth Stevens, Inc.

Franklin Watts series editor: Sarah Snashall
Franklin Watts editor: Jane Walker
Design: Visual Image
Artwork: Ruth Levy
Photography: Peter Millard

Additional photographs:
John Freeman/New Holland Publishers Ltd: 6 (top left); Carol Wills/Oxfam: 8 (top right); Robert Harding Picture Library: 14 (top left); Liz Clayton/Oxfam: 24 (top right).

Gareth Stevens editor: Jonny Brown
Gareth Stevens cover design: Kami Koenig

Very special thanks to Myra McDonnell, advisor and model maker.

Printed in the United States of America

1 2 3 4 5 6 7 8 9 08 07 06 05 04

Contents

The Art of Papercraft

Paper was probably invented in A.D. 105 by Tsai Lun, an official at the court of the Chinese emperor. Before that date, important information was written on strips of bamboo or silk. The popular new paper was made from the fibers of tree bark, hemp, or rags. It was cheap to make and light to carry.

Almost five hundred years after its discovery, paper was brought to Japan, via Korea, as the Buddhist religion spread across Asia. At first, paper was seen as a holy material and was used for written prayers or to make sacred banners. People soon realized that they could make many household items from paper, such as fans, umbrellas, bags, and lanterns. It could even be made into clothing, window coverings, and screens. During the eighth century A.D., craftsmen set up papermaking centers in Baghdad, Damascus, and Cairo, and from these places paper was imported into Europe. The first European papermaking centers were established in Spain. In 1690, the first paper mill was set up in the British colonies of North America. Papermaking quickly spread across the world.

The methods of making paper changed as new technologies were discovered. When Johannes Gutenberg invented printing in Germany in the 1400s, a new age of book publishing began. During the Industrial Revolution in Europe, paper was produced by machines. This change made the mass printing of newspapers and magazines possible. The first factory for machine-made paper opened in Shanghai, China, in 1892. The story of papermaking had come full circle to where it had begun almost two thousand years earlier.

Your Own Papermaking Kit

In this book you will find several ways to make and decorate your own paper and create items with it. Most of the equipment you will need is very simple and can be found around your home. You may want to collect some of those items and keep them in a papermaking kit. Here are some of the things you will need:

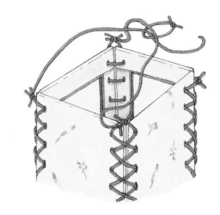

scissors • craft knife • metal ruler • brushes • paints • varnish • PVA (wood) glue • strong glue • clear tape •

masking tape • cardboard • paper • newspaper • pen • pencil • felt-tip pens • needle and thread • iron

papermaking mold

The first thing a papermaker needs is a mold. It is easy to make one from an old picture frame and a piece of window screen with a fine mesh.

Stretch the screen evenly over the frame. Make sure that the screen is tight and smooth and the corners are neat. Attach it around the edges with thumbtacks or a staple gun.

A secret watermark

A watermark is a hidden design or picture that is put into a sheet of paper while it is being made. You cannot see the watermark by just looking at the paper. Hold it up to the light and the watermark appears!

To make your own distinctive mark, bend a piece of thin wire into a shape. Sew this shape onto the surface of your paper mold with fine cotton thread. When you make your paper (see page 9), the watermark will be hidden in each sheet.

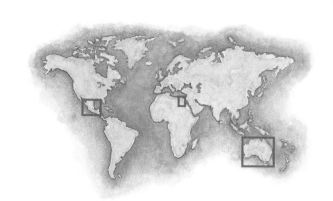

Papyrus and Bark

Before paper was invented, people wrote important records on pieces of pottery, wet clay, animal skin, or waxed wooden tablets. In China, early books were made by sewing together strips of bamboo. The word "paper" comes from papyrus, a reed that was first used by the ancient Egyptians to make paper. Strips of the reed are laid across each other and rolled until they fuse together to form a thin, strong paper (bottom right). The picture of Pharaoh Tutankhamun (below right) is painted on papyrus.

The Aboriginal peoples of Australia paint on tree bark. They strip the bark, soak it in water, and then heat it over a fire to make it pliable. The decorated bark-paper bag (left) is made by the Tiwi people who live off the coast of Australia. It is called a *tunga* and is worn for funeral ceremonies.

In Mexico, bark paper (below left) is made by the Otomi people of San Pablito. The hard, outer layer of bark is separated from the inner fibers, which are used for the paper, and the birds and flowers are painted by hand.

Make a Bark Painting

You can paint pictures on pieces of soaked and flattened bark, or on paper made from bark fibers. The flat sheets of cork that are used for floors and bulletin boards are made from the bark of the cork-oak tree. This bark makes an ideal surface for painting.

You will need: sheet of cork or cork tile (unvarnished) ▪ masking tape ▪ wooden board ▪ tracing paper ▪ pencil ▪ felt-tip pen ▪ acrylic paint in white, ochre (dirty yellow), burnt sienna (rust brown), and burnt umber (dark brown) ▪ paintbrush ▪ stick

4 Paint flat areas with a brush. Use your fingers or the end of a stick to form the dot pattern. Allow the piece to dry.

3 Tape tracing paper to the cork, and pencil over the lines. Go over the traced outline with a felt-tip pen.

Add a background pattern.

1 Tape the corners of the cork sheet or tile onto a board to keep it from moving or rolling up.

2 Find an idea from a book on art, or copy a picture of an animal like the opossum from Tasmania shown here. Draw your design on tracing paper. Turn the paper over and pencil over the lines on the back.

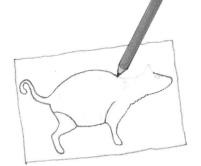

India, Japan, China, and Bangladesh

Handmade Paper

Most paper is made from plant fibers that are matted together to form a thin sheet and then dried flat. The first papers were made in China from tree bark, hemp plants, or cotton rags. Most of the paper we use today comes from wood pulp. The plants are pounded so that their fibers break into shorter lengths. The soft flesh of the plant is then washed away, and the fibers are added to water to form a "soup" that is strained through a mesh made of wire, fabric, or bamboo strips as seen above. The orange paper (below, far left) is made from rough coconut fibers. The papers and box of envelopes (below, left and center) are made in India. Petals, leaves, seeds, and even gold threads have been added as decoration. The nearly transparent papers on the right come from Japan and China. They contain long, shiny silk threads. The three tiny photo frames are made of hyacinth paper that comes from a women's cooperative in southern Bangladesh. The water hyacinth clogs up the waterways of Bangladesh, allowing malaria-carrying mosquitoes to multiply. By using that plant, the cooperative is helping both the local community and the papermakers.

Make Your Own Paper

The blue paper is made from newspaper and food coloring. White envelopes were used for the second paper. Pressed leaves were added for decoration.

You could add a watermark to your handmade paper. This method of marking paper was invented in Italy in the thirteenth century. The marks may have been a way of identifying the work of each papermaker.

You will need: used paper ▪ bucket ▪ food processor ▪ jug ▪ large plastic tub ▪ wooden spoon ▪ rubber gloves ▪ mold (see page 5) ▪ pressed leaves or petals ▪ tub ▪ tray ▪ newspaper ▪ tea towels or dishcloths ▪ heavy weight ▪ iron

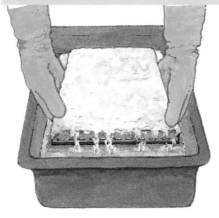

5 Place another tub upside down on the tray, and lay newspaper over it. Cover it with cloth. Turn the mold and gently transfer the drained pulp onto the cloth.

6 Continue building a pile of cloths and paper. Place a heavy weight on top. Let the pile dry, or iron each sheet dry between cloths. Peel away the cloths to remove the paper.

3 Pour one jugful of pulp and four jugfuls of water into a large plastic tub. Stir. Dip the mold, screen side up, into the bowl. Lift up gently, catching a thick layer of pulp on the screen.

4 Add petals or leaves for decoration. Allow the paper to drain.

1 Tear used paper into small squares. Soak it overnight in a bucket of water.

2 Using a food processor or electric blender, process the soaked paper in small amounts until it is a pulpy soup. Add plenty of water, and operate the machine in short bursts.

Papier-Mâché

As the invention of paper spread around the world, people from many countries found different ways of using it. They found that wet paper pulp or strips could be molded into any shape. When the finished product is painted and varnished, it becomes almost as stiff and hard-wearing as wood. This technique became known by the French name *papier-mâché*, which literally means "mashed paper."

The green and gold tray on the right was made in France. It represents the European tradition of papier-mâché, while the large bowl (bottom right) is an example of traditional Indian papier-mâché. The people of India's Kashmir region have been producing papier-mâché items since the fifteenth century. Today, beautifully painted pieces like the jewelry box and the cat (below) are still produced in the region. Other areas of the world also produce colorful papier-mâché. The bus (top right), called a *tap tap*, comes from Haiti. The melon-shaped tray (right center) comes from Mexico.

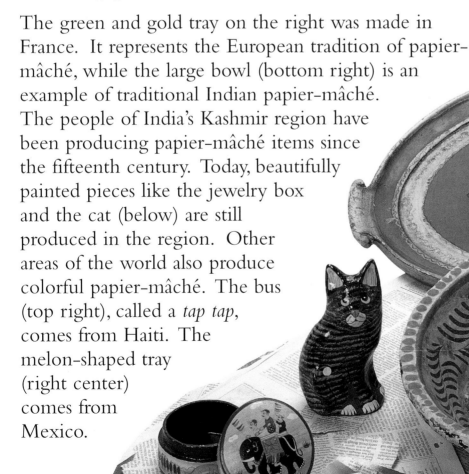

Make a Papier-Mâché Tray

There are two main methods of making papier-mâché. Most of the articles shown opposite were made by pasting strips or squares of paper onto a base or mold. You could use papier-mâché pulp, however, for the large tray. It is easy to make and can be molded rather like clay.

You will need: newspaper ▪ bucket ▪ water ▪ food processor ▪ 3 tablespoons flour ▪ large wooden spoon ▪ large plate or tray (for mold) ▪ plastic wrap ▪ white latex paint ▪ brushes ▪ pencil ▪ white paper ▪ acrylic paints ▪ varnish

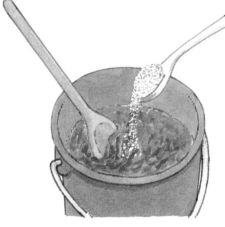

1 Prepare a thick pulp from newspaper using method shown in steps 1 and 2 on page 9. Add flour to the pulp, and mix well to form a soft "dough."

2 Turn the mold upside down. Cover it with plastic wrap to keep the papier-mâché from sticking.

3 Take a handful of pulp. Squeeze out the water. Pat it down onto the plastic wrap. Repeat this step to build a layer 1 inch thick. Smooth the pulp all over the mold.

4 Leave the mold in a warm, dry place for several days. When it is completely dry, gently pull the tray off the mold.

5 Brush white latex paint over the tray, and then apply a coat of colored paint. Plan a design, and draw it on the tray. Paint the design, and varnish your tray.

Marbling

Marbling is a simple but effective method of decorating paper. It involves adding oil-based paint to water. Oil floats on water, so the oil-based paint stays on the water's surface. The technique is called marbling because the pattern formed on the paper looks like the veins in polished marble. Marbling has traditionally been used to decorate the endpapers of hand-bound books.

The example below left was made in Britain over a century ago. It shows the typical dark, feathered patterns that are produced when a comb is dragged across the paint on the water's surface. In Bangladesh, the women who work at the Concern project (see page 8) decorate their paper with marbling. The packaging for these incense sticks (below right) was made from a sheet of marbled paper produced by these women. The marbled papers (below center) come from a factory in Pondicherry in southern India. Rich patterns are created with paint or ink. The pencil pot is covered with marbled paper to which a little gold paint has been added.

Simple Hand Marbling

You will need: plastic tray (large enough for a sheet of paper) ▪ water ▪ oil paints (at least two colors) ▪ two small cups ▪ turpentine ▪ brushes ▪ paper ▪ newspaper

This method uses ordinary oil paint and turpentine. Special marbling inks are available, however, at many craft shops.

1 Fill the tray with water.

2 Squeeze .75 inch of oil paint into a cup. Add 2 tsp of turpentine and mix well. Repeat this step with a different color in the second cup.

3 To test the paint, load some on a brush, and flick paint onto the water's surface. If the paint shrinks and sinks, add more turpentine. If it spreads too thinly, add more paint.

4 Clean the tray and refill it with water. Flick two different colors onto the surface. Drag the paint into swirls with the end of the brush.

5 Place paper gently on the surface. Leave it there for a few seconds, and then peel it off. Lay it flat to dry. Make a second print for a paler version. (Remove the paint from the water with a sheet of newspaper before beginning again.)

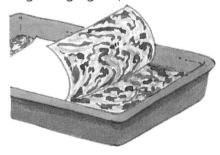

13

Papery Blooms

Flowers are often used to greet people and make places beautiful. Flower garlands are a traditional form of welcome in many of the islands of French Polynesia in the Pacific Ocean (see left). When real flowers are expensive or difficult to find, paper ones are a useful alternative. In Europe, rose petals were tossed on the floor for kings or victors of battles to walk on. Today, paper confetti (below) is thrown over bridal couples. Some confetti is still made in the shape of rose petals.

In Thailand, flowers are made from mulberry paper. They come in every shape and form, from lifelike roses to exotic jungle flowers (far left and below right). The paper is cut into petal shapes, which are soaked in water. Powder paint is then applied with water so the color spreads over the petals. Thin wires are glued down the center of each petal. White arum lilies grow wild in South America. The large one shown below is made from papier-mâché. The small decorative lilies in the pot are made from crêpe paper.

Make a Brilliant Bouquet

You will need: cardboard ▪ pencil ▪ scissors ▪ white crêpe paper ▪ PVA glue ▪ brush ▪ colored inks ▪ water ▪ thin wire ▪ cotton thread

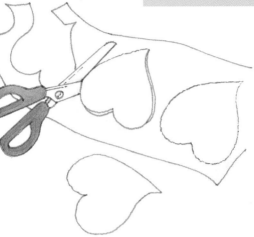

1 Draw a petal shape on cardboard, and cut it out. Lay the pattern on crêpe paper, and draw around the edge three times for each flower. Cut out the petals.

2 Apply glue at the edge of one petal. Lay a second petal over the first and apply more glue. Lay a third petal on top. Leave it to dry. Trim around the edges to make them neat.

3 Paint colored ink around the edge of the flower. Blend the color into the crêpe paper with clean water.

4 Cut 4 inches of wire. Wrap a strip of crêpe paper around it, and then glue it. Add extra paper at one end for the stamen. Paint the stalk green and the stamen yellow.

5 Wrap the petal around the base of the stamen. Secure it with glue and cotton thread. Bend the edges of the petal outward.

Repeat steps 1–5 to make more flowers for a bouquet.

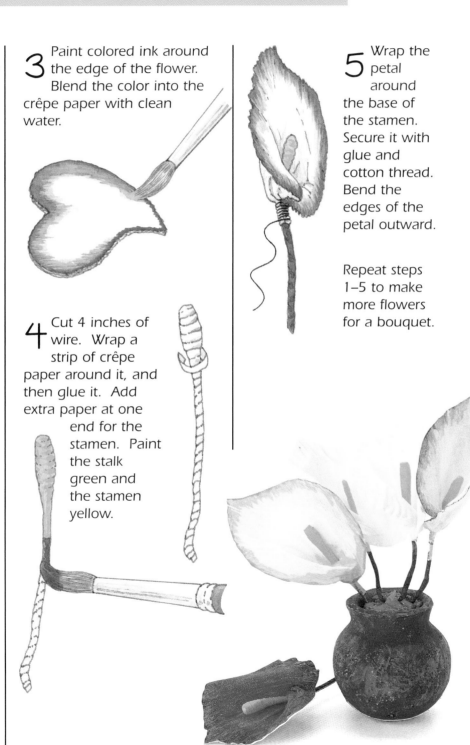

15

Paper Fans

A fan is a very simple and useful item. You can carry it folded, yet it opens up into a large area of paper that moves cool air over your face very efficiently. The paper fan may have been invented in China or Japan, where it was used by both men and women. At the Japanese imperial court, fans became a symbol of power. A fan is also the most important item carried by an actor in Japanese traditional Nō drama. Fans from the Far East have traditionally been made from bamboo strips with paper stretched over them. The two larger fans on the left come from China. They are decorated with painted birds and flowers. The fan idea can also be developed into even more decorative forms, like the butterfly above.

At one time in Europe, ladies owned a fan to match each dress. They used fans to hide their face and express their feelings. In time, a complete world of social etiquette grew up around the use of fans. They were made from luxurious materials, such as ivory, silk, and ostrich feathers, as well as from paper. They were often decorated with paintings, as this Victorian fan (bottom left) shows.

Make a Fantastic Fan

You will need: large sheet of wrapping paper ▪ large sheet of plain paper ▪ masking tape ▪ large wooden board ▪ pencil ▪ ruler ▪ cotton thread ▪ straight pin ▪ scissors ▪ stiff black cardboard ▪ small hole punch ▪ large bead ▪ thin wire, 6 inches long ▪ 2 two-holed buttons ▪ strong glue ▪ ribbon

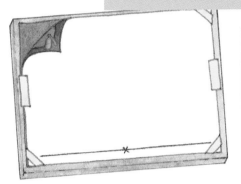

1 Tape both sheets of paper to the board. Draw a line 1.5 inches from one long edge. Mark a point halfway along it.

2 Tie the thread to the pencil to make a compass. Measure 10 inches along the thread and tie a knot. Push the pin through the knot and into the point marked on the paper. Use the compass to draw a semicircle.

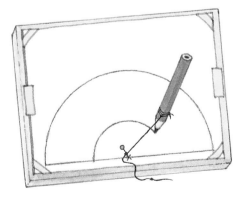

Repeat with a length of thread measuring 2.75 inches. Cut out the arch shape from both sheets of paper.

3 Cut 12 strips of black cardboard, 12 x .5 inches, for ribs. Punch a hole 2 inches from the base of each rib.

4 Thread the bead onto the wire. Bend the wire in half, and thread the ends through the button.

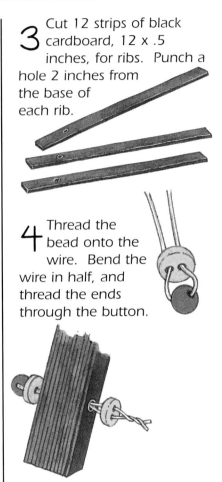

Push the wire through the ribs. Add a second button. Twist the wire loosely and trim the ends.

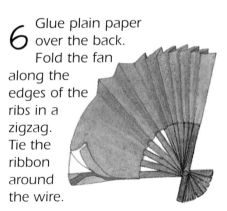

5 Place the wrapping paper face down. Lay the fanned-out ribs on top. Glue each rib end .75 inches from the edge of the paper. Fold the end of the paper over the rib, and glue it. Glue the ribs at equal intervals.

6 Glue plain paper over the back. Fold the fan along the edges of the ribs in a zigzag. Tie the ribbon around the wire.

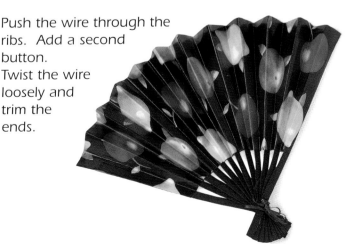

Lights and Lanterns

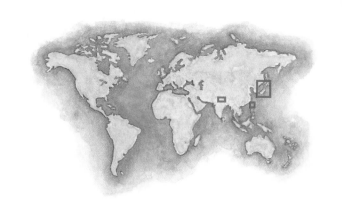

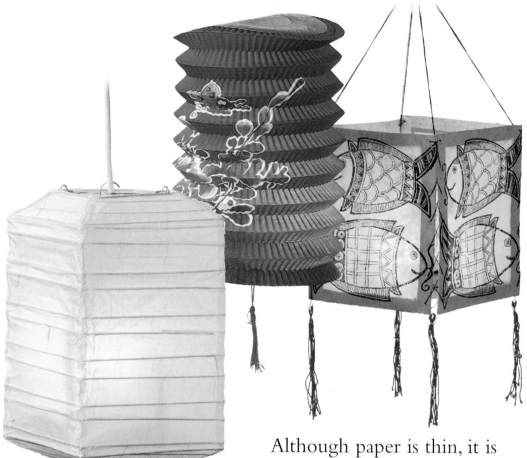

Although paper is thin, it is strong and light in weight. For this reason, it is an ideal material for lamp shades. Paper lanterns, which were probably invented in Japan, are now popular all over the world. The lampshade from Japan (above left) is made from paper that contains strands of silk. The Lantern Festival marks the end of the Chinese New Year celebrations. The colorful lantern (above center) was bought especially for the festival at a market stall in Taiwan. The simple white lantern from Tibet (above right) is decorated with fish — a symbol of freedom from the problems of the world.

Make a Paper Lantern

When this lantern is lit, it shows off the beauty of the handmade paper. You could copy the Tibetan lantern and paint the paper with a fish pattern, or you could use another design.

You will need: four pieces of cardboard, 5.5 x 7 inches • pencil • metal ruler • craft knife • four pieces of handmade paper, 6.5 x 8 inches • strong glue • modelng clay • awl • thin ribbon • large needle • scissors

1 Draw a rectangle .5 inch from the edges of the cardboard. Use the ruler and craft knife to cut away the center and leave a frame.

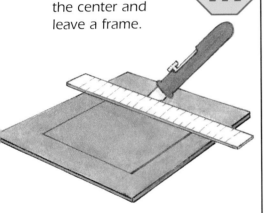

2 Place the frame in the center of a piece of handmade paper, and glue it. Fold the paper edges over the frame and glue them. Repeat steps 1–2 for three more frames.

3 Mark dots at intervals on the long sides of each frame, as shown. Hold the frames over modeling clay, and pierce a hole at each dot with an awl.

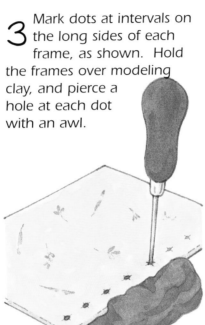

4 Place two frames together, with the right sides facing out. Using thin ribbon, loosely sew up one side and down again. Knot the ends. Attach the third and fourth frames in the same way to make a box shape.

5 Tie two long ribbons to the ribbons at opposite corners. To hang the lantern, attach a small loop of ribbon around the long ribbons.

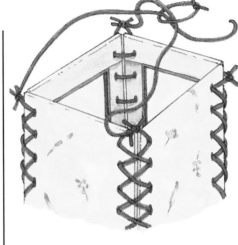

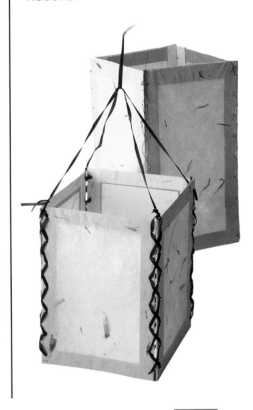

Bags and Cards

The art of gift wrapping is not new. Before plastic bags were introduced, most people carried their shopping home in paper bags. In India, bags are made out of spare paper. When you go to the market to buy eggs, they are given to you in a handmade newspaper bag like the one shown bottom right.

In many countries, the simple paper bag has developed into a sophisticated shopping bag. Shopping bags can be made from handmade paper, like the one below, or brightly printed with a design or advertisement. The two bags on the right and far right were made in Britain to advertise a museum and a shop. Paper bags are better for the environment than plastic bags, especially if they are made from recycled paper.

Gift tags and cards are one way in which paper is used to send greetings. The card on the right is from Sri Lanka. It is made from handmade paper and pressed wildflowers.

Make Your Own Gift Bag

The most useful paper bag to make is a gift bag. A present that is difficult to wrap can easily be popped into a gift bag. You can make any size bag once you have mastered the technique. Try making plain bags that you decorate yourself. Use them to advertise your school or club, or write a special message on the bag for the person who will receive the gift.

You will need: gift-wrap paper, 28 x 20 inches ▪ ruler ▪ strong glue ▪ two strips of cardboard, 1.5 x 10.5 inches ▪ hole punch ▪ colored cord

1 Fold in a 1.5-inch border on one long edge of the paper.

2 Overlap the shorter sides by .5 inch. Glue them to form a paper tube.

3 Fold the paper along the seam, and press the tube flat.

4 Mark a line 3 inches from the folded edge. Open the tube and fold it again at the 3-inch mark. Press the tube flat again. Fold both 3-inch sections in half, inwards.

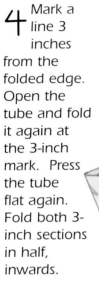

5 Fold up the bottom of the tube 3 inches from the edge.

Open it again.

Fold the short sides in and crease them.

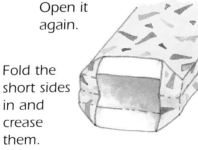

Fold the top flap down and the bottom flap up. Glue them in place.

6 Slip strips of cardboard under the top cuff on both sides. Punch four holes through the cuff and the cardboard. Thread cord handles through the holes, and knot it on the inside.

Paper Cutting

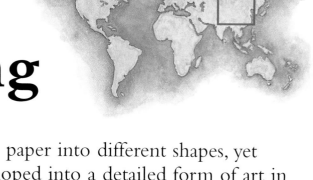

It is not difficult to cut paper into different shapes, yet paper-cutting has developed into a detailed form of art in many countries. The colorful cutouts at the foot of this page represent traditional Chinese characters. They are cut from fine tissue paper that is then painted. The single-color cutouts of Biblical figures and stories (below left) are made by Fan Pu of the Amity Christian Art Center in Nanjing, China.

In Europe, traditional patterns of paper cutting followed the designs painted on peasant furniture. The round paper cutout of two roosters (left) comes from Poland. It is not painted but is made of layers of different colored paper. During the 1500s, a craze of silhouette paper-cutting took Europe by storm. A candle was placed beside the subject to throw a shadow onto a piece of paper on the wall. The artist then traced the profile, filling it in with ink. In France, this was seen as a poor substitute for a painted portrait so the method was named after a much-hated aristocrat, Etienne de Silhouette. By the 1800s, a machine had been invented that shrank the shadow so miniature portraits could be made. The miniature portrait at the top left was hand cut in Britain around 1950, when silhouettes were still popular.

Make a Portrait Silhouette

Here is a modern way of making a portrait silhouette. You may also want to try the original method, using a candle to cast the shadow of your sitter onto the wall. You can make the sitter look like a historic person by adding a period hat or a crown!

You will need: large photograph of someone in profile ▪ tracing paper ▪ masking tape ▪ pencil ▪ white paper ▪ black ink ▪ pen ▪ brush ▪ oval-shaped cardboard mount ▪ photo frame

3 Tape the tracing paper to the white paper, and transfer the traced profile (see page 7). Take care to be accurate so you do not spoil the likeness.

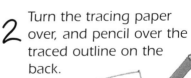

1 Tape tracing paper over the photograph. Trace lightly around the profile with a pencil.

2 Turn the tracing paper over, and pencil over the traced outline on the back.

4 Carefully go over the outline with ink.

5 Fill in the whole shape with black ink.

6 Tape your picture onto the mount and place it inside the frame to make it look like a professional portrait.

Pinwheels

When you make a sand castle on the beach, it is complete only when crowned with a pinwheel. This paper toy makes use of the wind to whirl itself around, like a windmill. The pinwheels below were bought at an English beach resort. They are made from light plastic, not paper.

No one knows where pinwheels came from. They may have developed from pieces of paper hung up to scare birds away from crops or from devices that sailors used to figure out the speed of the wind. Small metal pinwheels are still used to check the wind speed on the ground at airports.

In India, many types of toys are made of paper, and paper pinwheels are very popular. These women (right) are making masks and decorations. They have also made a pinwheel.

Make a Pinwheel Toy

Here is a method of making a single pinwheel. You could make several and attach them to a frame like the one shown here.

You will need: square of stiff colored paper ▪ pencil ▪ ruler ▪ scissors ▪ long, round-headed map pin ▪ two beads ▪ clear tape ▪ wooden plant stick

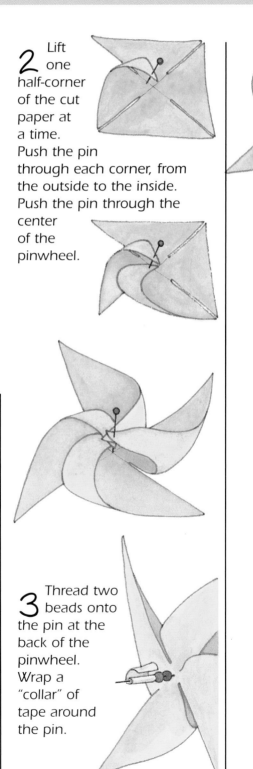

2 Lift one half-corner of the cut paper at a time. Push the pin through each corner, from the outside to the inside. Push the pin through the center of the pinwheel.

4 Push the pin into the wooden stick, near the top. Make sure that it whirls around freely.

3 Thread two beads onto the pin at the back of the pinwheel. Wrap a "collar" of tape around the pin.

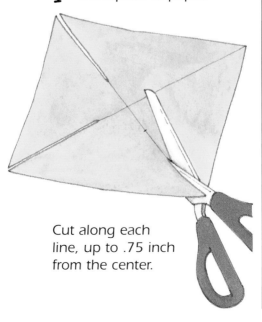

1 Mark diagonal lines on the square of paper.

Cut along each line, up to .75 inch from the center.

Bookbinding

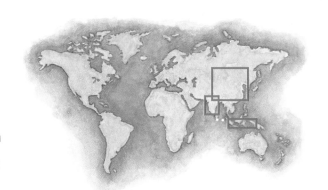

When people wanted to keep an important set of pages together in a manuscript, they had to invent a way of keeping all the writing in one place. The earliest writing was done on clay or wooden boards and, later, on long rolls of papyrus or leather, called scrolls. Around the second century AD, the scroll began to be replaced by a pile of folded paper sheets that were sewn together at one edge. This technique may have been invented by early Christians, so they could carry their precious manuscripts around safely. Today, good-quality printed books are still sewn together at the spine. Handmade papers are bound into books in the same way.

Small papermaking cooperatives make beautiful gift books for sale around the world. The hand-sewn gift book (below center) comes from Indonesia and is threaded with cord made from twisted paper. The book with the fish motif (below left) comes from India, and the simpler workman's notebook (right) is from China. The notebook with the bamboo strip to close it (bottom right) is from Nepal. The paper comes from the bark of the lokta tree, which regrows quickly. Use of this bark helps to preserve the forests.

Make a Simple Sewn Book

You could use construction paper (a less expensive choice than handmade paper) for the inside sheets of your book.

You will need: 2 pieces of cardboard, 8.25 x 5.75 inches ▪ craft knife ▪ metal ruler ▪ 2 sheets of handmade paper, 9 x 6.5 inches ▪ strong glue ▪ scissors ▪ 20 sheets of construction paper, 7.5 x 5 inches ▪ string ▪ newspaper ▪ awl ▪ hammer ▪ thin ribbon ▪ large needle

1 To make the front cover, use a craft knife and ruler to cut a .1-inch strip and a .75-inch strip off the edge of one piece of cardboard. Throw away the .1-inch strip.

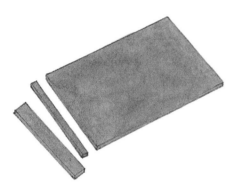

2 Glue the cardboard and the .75-inch strip (for the hinge) in the center of one sheet of handmade paper. Cut the corners off the paper to prevent overlapping. Fold the paper over the cardboard.

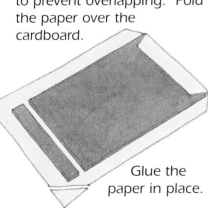

Glue the paper in place.

3 Glue a sheet of construction paper inside to complete the front cover. Repeat steps 1–3 for the back cover, without cutting off cardboard strips for a hinge.

4 Stack the book with the front cover on top. Tie it together with string.

5 Lay the book on a pile of newspapers. Use an awl and a hammer to punch a line of five holes, .75 inch apart, through the cardboard and paper.

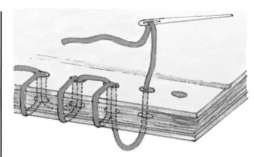

6 Thread the ribbon on a needle, and sew down through the first hole. Wrap the ribbon around the spine edge, and go down through the same hole again. Sew up through the next hole and repeat the process to the end.

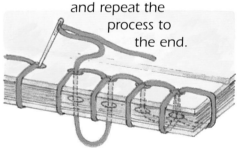

Bring the last stitch up around the side of the book. Sew down and up along the holes, filling in gaps. Tie a bow. Remove the string.

Origami

In Japan, the art of folding paper is called origami. Below, on the right, are some traditional origami figures: the boat, the frog, the crab, and the duck. Many of the traditional shapes are very complicated, and people work for years to become good origamists.

The crane (below left) is a fairly simple design. Most Japanese children learn to make it at home or in school. The crane is a symbol of long life and loyalty. It also represents the soul of a person. It has come to be associated with peace and with the commemoration of the terrible end to World War II, when atomic bombs were dropped on the cities of Hiroshima and Nagasaki. On the anniversary of this event in August each year, children make strings of small paper cranes (bottom left). They hang them in their homes in memory of those who died and in the hope that such a tragedy will never happen again.

Make an Origami Hat

You will need to follow these steps carefully. Crease along each fold with your fingernail to make the folds very exact.

If you want to make more origami figures, look for a book on the subject in your school or local library.

You will need: a square of origami paper or gift wrap (to make your own hat to wear, you will need a square about 16 x 16 inches)

1 Fold the square in half to form a rectangle. Fold the rectangle in half and crease it.

2 Open the rectangle and fold the sides in towards the middle.

3 Open the leaf on each side. Fold the top down to form triangles and crease.

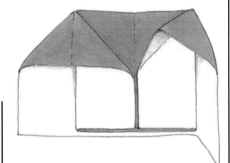

4 Fold both ends around to the back.

5 Fold up the bottom half of the front three times to form a cuff.

6 Turn the hat over and fold up the bottom half of the back three times.

Pull the hat open and make a dent in the top.

Glossary

aristocrat: a member of a small, select group of people who govern a country or area

arum lilies: members of the lily family that grow wild in South America and have large, showy flowers

Buddhist: a follower of the religion started in India by Gautama Buddha

confetti: small pieces of colored paper that are scattered over the newly married couple at a wedding

cooperatives: groups of people who work together, sharing materials, a workplace, and profits from their work

endpapers: special sheets of paper that are stuck into the beginning and end of a book

etiquette: the accepted way to behave towards other people

fibers: thin strands or threads that are used to make a material or fabric

hemp: a woody plant whose fibers are used to make rope

jute: a glossy plant fiber used to make burlap and twine

lokta tree: a fast-growing tree, found in Nepal, that is used for making paper

manuscript: a document that is written by hand; also refers to an author's text for a new book, whether typed or handwritten

marbling: a design or form of decoration that is made to look like a piece of marble

mesh: fine strands of a screen that are placed at right angles to each other, with tiny, open spaces in between

mount: the cardboard to which a picture is attached for framing

mulberry paper: paper that is made from the leaves of the mulberry tree

Nō drama: a form of traditional Japanese theatre

origami: the Japanese art of folding paper to make shapes

papier-mâché: a craft material made from glue and scraps of paper or paper pulp

papyrus: paper that is made from the stems of the papyrus plant

pliable: bendable or easily reshaped

powder paint: a dry form of paint that is mixed with a liquid before or during application

profile: a side view of something, especially a person's face

pulp: a soft, shapeless mass of rags, wood and other material. It is used to make paper.

scrolls: ancient books made from a long strip of rolled paper

silhouette: a shadow or outline of a person or thing

watermark: an invisible mark in a sheet of paper that can help identify the papermaker

More Books to Read

Easy Origami. John Montroll (Dover)

Making Magic Windows: Creating Cut-Paper Art with Carmen Lomas Garza. Carmen Lomas Garza (Children's Book Press)

Papercrafts Around the World. Phyllis Fiarotta, Noel Fiarotta (Sterling)

Papermaking for Kids: Simple Steps to Handcrafted Paper. Beth Wilkinson (Gibbs Smith)

Papermaking. Step by Step. David Watson (Heinemann Library)

Web Sites

Crafts for Kids
http://www.craftforkids.co.uk/

Magical Kingdom: Paper Craft Listing
http://www.magicalkingdom.co.uk/craftlisting.htm

Papier Mâché
http://www.tpt.org/donnasday/creative/activ14.html

Paper University: Art Class
http://www.tappi.org/paperu/art_class/makingPaper.htm

Index